Listen and Draw

Easy Drawing Activities for the EFL/ESL Classroom

A Teacher's Resource Book

NEW EDITION

Stephen Mark Silvers
Retired, Federal University of Amazonas
Manaus, Amazonas, Brazil

Listen and Draw: Easy Drawing Activities for the EFL/ESL Classroom: A Teacher's Resource Book.
New Edition

Copyright © by Stephen Mark Silvers, 2018

All rights reserved. No part of this book may be used or reproduced in any manner whatsoever for commercial purposes. However, permission is hereby granted for teachers to reproduce the exercises for use in their classrooms.

Cover design by Grace Rajendran
Illustrations by the author

ISBN: 978-0-692-14354-4

Contents

- **A.** Quick guide to the units **1**
- **B.** Detailed guide to the units **2**
- **C.** Introduction **4**
- **D.** Appendices
    1. More things to draw **123**
    2. Erase **126**
    3. Practice some more **127**
    4. Pairwork language **129**
    5. List of nouns **130**
- **E.** Index of structures **131**
- **F.** Bibliography and additional resources **135**
- **G.** Acknowledgements **136**
- **H.** About the author **137**

Quick guide to the units

Unit 1	**Key Drawings** 19	
Unit 2	Look and Say for the Key Drawings 23	
Unit 3	Practice with the Key Drawings 27	
Unit 4	Preparatory for Five Positions 31	
Unit 5	Preparatory for Five Positions 35	
Unit 6	**Five Positions** 39	
Unit 7	Preparatory for Seven Positions 43	
Unit 8	**Seven Positions** 47	
Unit 9	Preparatory for Eleven Positions 51	
Unit 10	**Eleven Positions** 55	
Unit 11	Preparatory for Advanced Drawings-1 63	
Unit 12	Look and Say for Unit 11 67	
Unit 13	**Advanced Drawings-1** 73	
Unit 14	Preparatory for Advanced Drawings-2 85	
Unit 15	Look and Say for Unit 14 91	
Unit 16	Preparatory for Advanced Drawings-2 97	
Unit 17	Look and Say for Unit 16 101	
Unit 18	**Advanced Drawings-2** 109	

Detailed guide to the units

Unit 1	**Key Drawings**
Unit 2	Look and Say activities for the Key Drawings
Unit 3	A/an – Big/small – A/some/a few – There is/there are Noun plurals – It/they – It/them – Inside
Unit 4	In the center – At the top – At the bottom
Unit 5	Next to, on the left – Next to, on the right
Unit 6	**Five Positions** In the center – At the top – At the bottom Next to, on the left – Next to, on the right
Unit 7	Over – Under
Unit 8	**Seven Positions** In the center – At the top – At the bottom Next to, on the left – Next to, on the right Over – Under
Unit 9	Upper left-hand corner – Upper right-hand corner Lower left-hand corner – Lower right-hand corner
Unit 10	**Eleven Positions** In the center – At the top – At the bottom Next to, on the left – Next to, on the right Over – Under In the upper left-hand corner – In the upper right-hand corner In the lower left-hand corner – In the lower right-hand corner
Unit 11	Upside-down – Broken lines In front of – In back of *(behind)* – Around In *(inside)* – On *(on top of)* – Between – Next to *(beside)* Vocabulary to describe a face *(long hair, big nose)*

Unit 12	Look and Say activities for Unit 11
Unit 13	**Advanced Drawings-1** All eleven positions and the vocabulary from Unit 11
Unit 14	One/ones *(the big one)* – The other/the others One – The other – Both A few – Some – A lot of Beside – Inside – Around – Over – Under Between – On top of Ordinal numbers *(first)* – Lines *(curved line)* Shapes and symbols *(diamond, dollar sign)*
Unit 15	Look and Say activities for Unit 14
Unit 16	Has – Doesn't have – Any *(doesn't have any hair)* Comparatives with –ER *(bigger)* Superlatives with –EST *(the biggest)* A little – A lot – Much *(a little bigger)* ING phrases *(the man wearing a hat)* Present progressive *(He's wearing a hat.)* Clothing *(skirt, tie)* – The face *(nose, ear)*
Unit 17	Look and Say activities for Unit 16
Unit 18	**Advanced Drawings-2** Structures and vocabulary from units 11, 14, and 16 Some new vocabulary introduced in each of the ten drawings

Introduction

Listen and Draw is an EFL/ESL teacher's resource book of simple, ready-to-use classroom drawing activities that can be used to:

- provide a quick filler
- supplement and enrich a lesson
- add variety and provide a change of pace

These activities, in which the students make simple drawings according to verbal instructions, develop the important skill of **listening comprehension.** Also, many of the activities can be used for pairwork, in which case the students will be practicing **speaking.**

These drawing activities had their beginning in 1978 as part of a Total Physical Response (TPR)* approach to teaching English as a foreign language to university students in Brazil. In 1985 they were incorporated into my book *Listen and Perform,* and in 2000 into *Listen and Act,* a book used to teach English in the Amazonas state middle schools. For information about the TPR approach to language instruction, see Bibliography and Additional Resources, page 135.

The drawings

The drawings are all very simple: no artistic skill or talent is needed. In any case, my drawings can be used as a model if so desired. But, of course, you and your students are free to make your own versions of the things to be drawn. In fact, that will make the activity more interesting and more fun. Here are examples of three drawings that are used early in the materials.

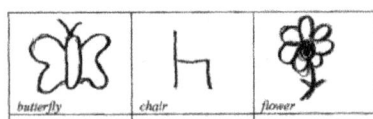

---

* Total Physical Response is an approach to language instruction based on the use of actions, such as opening the door, shaking hands, walking to the board, etc.

In later units some of the drawings contain more details, but they are still easy to draw, as for example:

Many of the exercises require the students to draw a big rectangle and then draw things in different locations inside it. Below is an example from Unit 6, which uses five locations or positions.

    Draw a big rectangle.
        1. In the center, draw a house.
        2. At the top, draw a circle.
        3. At the bottom, draw a heart.
        4. Next to the house, on the left, draw an umbrella.
        5. Next to the house, on the right, draw a ruler.

This is an easy drawing and is thus appropriate for beginners; however, there is a progression from easier to more difficult, and the drawings gradually become more complex.

Introduction

Organization of the materials

The materials have been organized into 18 units, each of which contains a number of ready-to-use classroom drawing activities. Six of the units form a progression of increasingly more complex drawings, and taken together they form the core of the materials. These six **key units** are as follows:

>**Unit 1** *(Key drawings)*
>
>**Unit 6** *(Five Positions)*
>
>**Unit 8** *(Seven Positions)*
>
>**Unit 10** *(Eleven Positions)*
>
>**Unit 13** *(Advanced Drawings-1)*
>
>**Unit 18** *(Advanced Drawings-2)*

In the Quick Guide to the Units and the Detailed Guide to the Units, these six key units have been signaled by bold type. In the book, these key units are signaled by ➔   The other units are "preparatory" units: they present and practice the vocabulary and structures that will be used in subsequent key units.

Lexical coverage

These materials use a limited number of vocabulary items. There are several factors that contributed to and/or limited my selection of lexical items. In the first place, an object (*heart*) or an action (*crying*) had to be something that could be drawn both easily and quickly. A second consideration was that fewer vocabulary items meant that they could be better recycled throughout the materials. A final consideration was the fact that vocabulary development is not an aim of these materials.

Unit 1 presents the 36 **key drawings** that form the basis for the activities in Unit 6 (five positions), Unit 8 (seven positions), and Unit 10 (eleven positions). More vocabulary is added in Units 11, 14, 16, and 18. Appendix 5, page 130, is a list of all the nouns used, with the unit of their first appearance. Other drawings that you may wish to include can be found in Appendix 1 (More Things to Draw), page 123. For published resources with simple drawings, see Bibliography and Additional Resources, page 135.

Introduction

Grammatical coverage and fluency practice

It should be emphasized that the aim of these materials is neither to teach nor to practice grammar. The grammar structures have been chosen based on the ease with which they can be represented by a drawing. Thus, the structures most frequently used are prepositional phrases of location (*at the top*), participial phrases (*wearing a hat*), the present progressive (*he's crying*), and articles (*a hat, the sun*).

On the other hand, a major aim of these materials is to provide opportunities for **fluency practice** within a structured communicative framework. This is done by having the students work in pairs, where one of the two pairwork partners looks at a drawing and tells his or her partner what to draw. It is communicative because there is an information gap (only the speaker knows what the drawing looks like), and the drawer cannot reproduce the drawing unless the speaker's message has been successfully sent and received. It is structured because the students are working within a limited set of grammatical structures and vocabulary items. It has the potential to promote fluency because the more the students do an activity, the easier it becomes. With enough practice, the students will be able to "fill time with speech," that is, easily produce intelligible utterances one after another without excessive delays or hesitations, an ability which is considered to be an important component of fluency. In practice this means that if your goal is fluency you will sometimes need to repeat a pairwork activity over a period of several class meetings until the students can perform it easily.

However, this is not to say that you cannot use any of the activities to give your students extra grammar practice. The Index of Structures (page 131) lists all of the grammatical words and structures used. Next to each grammatical item you will find a number in bold type indicating the unit where it first appears and/or is given special focus. Sometimes it will be part of an activity that can be used for separate grammar practice, if so desired. Often, however, the item does not receive enough focus to justify using it as a supplementary grammar practice activity. For a resource with drawing activities to practice grammar, see *Complete English Grammar*

Introduction

on CD: *The Best Way to TPR any Grammatical Feature in English* in the Bibliography.

Position of the adverbial phrases of place

Adverbial phrases of place usually come at the end of the sentence[*]: *I'll meet you at the park. There's a star at the top.* However, for special emphasis or focus they can sometimes be placed at the beginning: *At the top, draw a star. At the top, there's a star.* This is especially true for descriptions (and in essence all of these drawing exercises are a type of description).

In Units 1-10, the adverbial phrase is always at the beginning. This draws attention to it and thus makes it more prominent or noticeable. It also means that the sentence will have two separate focal points: the adverbial phrase of location (at the beginning of the sentence) and the object to be drawn (at the end of the sentence). This dual or divided focus makes it easier for the students to process the information and facilitates their understanding of the spoken message.

Practice with adverbial phrases of location at the end of the sentence is given in the advanced drawings (Units 13 and 18).

Drawing	Position of the adverbial phrase
1, 2, 3, 4	at the beginning *At the top, draw a star.* *At the top, there's a star.*
5, 6, 7 8, 9, 10	at the beginning and at the end *At the top, draw a star.* *At the top, there's a star.* *Draw a star at the top.* *There's a star at the top.*

---

[*] This is a simplification, but it is accurate enough for our purposes.

Introduction

Ways the materials can be used

There are several possibilities for using these materials.

1. As short supplementary activities

Many, perhaps most, EFL/ESL teachers are locked into a school-chosen textbook that leaves little time for long extra activities. Most of the activities presented here, however, can be done fairly quickly (five to ten minutes) and can be used to bring variety, fun, and interest to the lesson. But bear in mind that the drawings in Unit 13 (Advanced Drawings-1) and Unit 18 (Advanced Drawings-2) are more complex and will take more time. For most teachers, the best and possibly the only option will be to use the book as a resource for short supplementary activities.

2. As a "fixed component" to develop listening comprehension

Time permitting, you could include a short listening/drawing activity on a regular basis. As the materials have been structured so that there is a progression from simpler to more complex, you can follow the units in the order presented, skipping any units that your students don't need. It would also be possible for a school/language institute to use the activities on a planned basis over two or more levels, stages, or semesters.

3. As a "fixed component" to develop both listening and speaking

This is the same as (2) above, except that you are also systematically planning for pairwork, which, of course, will take up more class time.

4. As a short intensive course for beginners to develop listening and speaking

This is the same as (3) above, except that rather than spreading the exercises out in short "installments" over a school term (or terms), the exercises are presented in a stand-alone, short intensive course of perhaps 20 hours (this can be expanded or contracted according to your needs). In this case, you might also want to include some language practice based on the drawings (see page 16).

Introduction

Before using options (2), (3) or (4), I suggest that you first become familiar with the materials by using them as short supplementary exercises as described in option (1).

Finding appropriate activities

Ideally the activities you do with your students will be at the appropriate level, neither too easy nor too difficult. (However, you may often find that an activity which you feel would be too easy for your students will in reality be worthwhile and much enjoyed!) For beginners or false beginners, I suggest that you follow the ordered sequence of the 18 units. There is a carefully planned progression in which each unit either consolidates a previous unit or prepares the students for the next level of drawing activities. For high beginners and intermediate level students, you can follow these steps:

1. *Go to the Detailed Guide to the Units.* This will show you at a glance the focus and the structures used in each unit.

2. *Examine each of the six Key Units, noting the contents of the "preparatory" unit or units that precede it.*

3. *Choose a unit that seems appropriate.* It could be a Key Unit or a "preparatory" unit.

4. *Go to that unit and examine the activities.*

5. *Select activities within that unit in accordance with your objectives and the class time you have at your disposal.*

However, if you are willing to invest a little more time, I suggest that you first examine both the Quick Guide to the Units and the Detailed Guide to the Units and then go through the book unit by unit, noting how appropriate each activity would be for your students. If possible, this should be done together with another teacher. Admittedly, this will take some time, but the hour or two spent will enable you to make the best use of the materials.

The basic procedure

The basic procedure is quite simple. You call one or two students up to the front board. Then you tell them and the students who are seated what to draw. Often you will want to first demonstrate by making your own drawing and having the students draw along with you, especially when you are presenting vocabulary and structures that are new.

      T: Draw a fish. *(perhaps demonstrating)*
      Ss: *(Students draw a fish.)*
      T: Draw a house.
      Ss: *(Students draw a house.)*

Frequently you will ask the students to draw a big rectangle and draw things inside it (see page 5).

      T: Draw a big rectangle.
      Ss: *(Students draw a rectangle.)*
      T: In the center, draw a house.
      Ss: *(Students draw a house in the center of their rectangle.)*
      T: At the top, draw a circle.
      Ss: *(Students draw a circle at the top of their rectangle.)*

You will usually want to have the students who are at the board (not those at their seats) erase what they drew. This can be done after each drawing.

      T: Draw a fish.
      Ss: *(Students draw a fish.)*
      T: Erase it.
      Ss: *(The students at the board erase the fish they drew.)*

Or it could be done after the students have produced several drawings.

      T: Erase the fish.
      Ss: *(The students at the board erase the fish they had drawn.)*
      T: Now erase the house.
      Ss: *(The students at the board erase the house they had drawn.)*

For more suggestions on how to incorporate commands with *erase* into your lessons, see Appendix 2, page 126.

Introduction

The activities

There are four types of activities:

1. Presentation *(page 12)*
2. Practice *(page 12)*
3. Look and Say *(page 15)*
4. Read and Say *(page 16)*

1. Presentation

This presents the focal point of the unit. You can:

- Present it yourself. You give a drawing command and at the same time make the drawing. The students at their seats draw along with you. You can also have one or two students at the board draw along with you.

- Call a student up front to do the drawing. The student does the drawing, but you provide help if needed.

2. Practice

These exercises are presented in the form of a substitution table:

Draw an upside-down | tree.*
                    | airplane.
                    | house.

This is a compact format that allows you to make several drawing commands from a single sentence.

T: Draw an upside-down tree.
Ss: *(Students draw.)*
T: Draw upside-down house.
Ss: *(Students draw.)*

---

* Do not always use the items from a substitution box in the same order as the words in the box. Vary the order so that the students cannot guess what you are going to say.

Sometimes the activity is a two-command series in which the second command is signaled by the symbol ■.

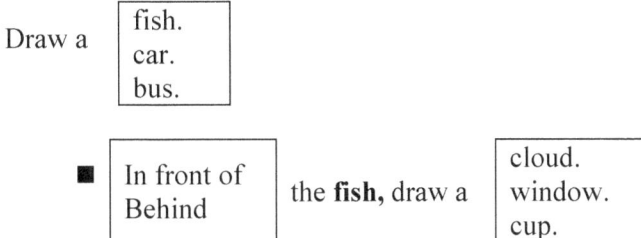

These exercises can take one of two forms:

A. *Command – Draw – Command – Draw*

You give the first command and the students draw. Then you give a second command.

    T: Draw a fish.
    Ss: *(Students draw a fish.)*
    T: In front of the fish *(it)*, draw a cup.
    Ss: *(Students draw a cup in front of the fish.)*

B. *Command – Command – Draw*

You give two commands, one right after the other. This is more difficult as the students must understand both commands and then hold them in their memory.

    T: Draw a fish. In front of the fish, draw a cup.
    Ss: *(Students draw a fish with a cup in front of it.)*

Note that sometimes the students actually need to hear the second command in order to make the drawing.

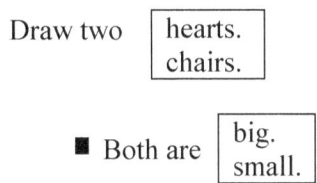

Introduction

Thus, in the above example, the students can only make the drawing when they know whether they are to draw two big hearts or two small ones. Also note that a declarative sentence can function as a command: *Both are big* = Make a drawing in which both objects are big.

When the students are instructed to draw a square/rectangle and draw things inside it, the **command groups** are numbered. When there are two or more items in a substitution box, as in (2) below, each item is used as a separate command.

Draw a square. *(Draw five squares.)**

1. In the center, draw a **window**.

2. | Over | the **window**, draw a **circle**.
   | Under |

   | window | fish | circle |
   | tree | flower | square |

Below is an example of the commands you could give for this activity. After each command you would pause while the students make their drawings. Again, note that (2) is actually two commands, one for *over,* and another for *under.*

Draw a square.
1. In the center, draw a window.
2. Over the window, draw a circle.
3. Under the window, draw a fish.

---

* **Tip:**
You could have the students draw several squares. That way, you wouldn't have to repeat "Draw a square" before each drawing.

Note also that the words **window** and **circle** are in bold type. This signals that they can be replaced and substituted by other words in the substitution box.

3. Look and Say

For these activities you choose a square/rectangle and dictate the drawing to your students. The activity below is the Look and Say version of the Practice activity above.

Choose a square and tell your students what to draw.

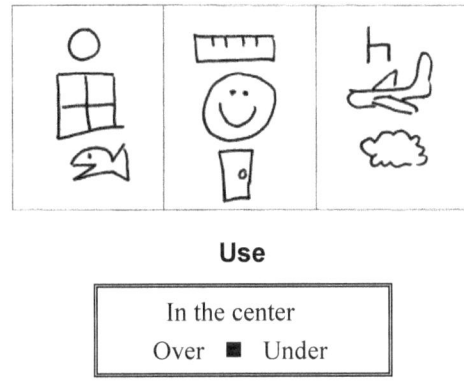

Use

| In the center |
| Over ■ Under |

Practice and Look and Say are essentially the same activity, but in different formats. Choose the format that you find easiest to use. (You may wish to begin with the substitution table as it has all of the verbal cues and then go to its corresponding graphic Look and Say version.)

In units 4-10, each Practice activity is immediately followed on the next page by corresponding Look and Say activities. In contrast, units 1, 11, 14, and 16 do not have Look and Say activities; they consist solely of a series of six or seven Practice activities, and the corresponding Look and Say activities are in the following unit (Units 2, 12, 15, and 17, respectively).

The exercises in these paired Practice /Look and Say units (1-2, 11-12, 14-15 and 16-17) have been cross-referenced so that you can do a Practice activity and then easily find its Look and Say version or vice-versa.

Introduction

The Look and Say activities are particularly well-suited for pairwork (see page 17). However, it will often be helpful if your students first see and repeat the written forms in the Practice activities.

4. Read and Say

In these activities, which are for Unit 13 (Advanced Drawings-1) and Unit 18 (Advanced Drawings-2), all of the commands are written out. First you have your students draw a big rectangle. Then you read the drawing commands, pausing after each one to give them time to make their drawings.

Some of the numbered commands in Unit 18 consist of more than one sentence. In the example below (from page 116) there are three sentences.

> 1. In the center, draw a sad face wearing a hat. It has small ears, a short beard, and a triangle for its nose. It has only one eye.

For these multi-sentence drawing commands, you first instruct your students to wait until you have read all of the sentences (in this example, three). Then you read the set of sentences, and say, "OK. Now you may draw." You may need to read the set of sentences more than once.

Using the drawings for language practice

Once a drawing is on the board, it can be used for language practice. This is particularly true for the six Key Units, but in most cases it can also apply to the preparatory activities. You can (1) make true/false statements, (2) practice questions and answers, (3) have the students describe the drawing, and (4) erase the drawing and have the students reconstruct it from memory. For examples of these activities, see Appendix 3 (Practice Some More), page 127. But keep in mind that they are OPTIONAL and will increase the class time spent on the activity.

Pairwork

All of the activities are well-suited for pairwork, and, if used CONSISTENTLY, they will lead to an increased level of fluency (see page 7). This is especially true for the drawing activities in the Key Units (signaled by bold type in the Quick Guide to the Units), but the Preparatory units can also be used effectively for pairwork. In addition to specific structures and vocabulary, various conversational language functions can also be practiced. For examples, see Appendix 4 (Pairwork Language).

For your convenience, all of the activities are available as a free PDF file which you can download, print and photcopy for your students. You need one copy of an activity for each pair, so if you have twenty students you only need ten handouts for that pairwork activity. Once printed, the copies can be stored in labelled manila envelopes for future use. Here is where you can find the handouts:

---
www.stephensilvers.academia.edu
click on
EFL Classroom Materials / Handouts for Listen and Draw

You will have to decide whether you want your students to use the **Practice** activities (see page 12) or the **Look and Say** activities (see page 15). The Look and Say activities are more demanding as the speaking cues are drawings and not words, which means that the students must supply the words from memory.

There are four options for using the **Read and Say** activites (Units 13 and 18) for pairwork: (1) the speaker reads the sentences; (2) the speaker reads a sentence silently to himself, looks up at his partner, and says the sentence from memory, referring back to the handout if necessary; (3) the speaker silently reads all of the sentences, covers them up, looks at the drawing, and tells his partner what to draw; and (4) the speaker covers the written sentences, looks at the drawing, and tells his partner what to draw.

Introduction

Procedures for pairwork

1. Do the actitity with the class. Before you use an activity for pairwork, the students should already have done it one or more times as a teacher-led activity in which they drew from your commands. If the students have had enough previous teacher/class practice, you can skip this step and go directly to the pairwork activity itself.
2. Arrange the students in pairs.
3. Distribute the handout(s).
4. Do a teacher/class repetition of sentences that will be used in the activities. (This is optional, but it is usually helpful.)
5. Walk around the class, providing help as needed.

A final word

I hope that you will find these activities useful and that they will stimulate your own creativity in the teaching of English as a foreign or second language.

As a final suggestion, you can take the book to a local printing establishment and have them cut the spine and rebind the book with a spiral coil. I often did this with course books when I was teaching English in Brazil and always found that it made them much easier to use in class. I highly recommend this.

Unit 1

Key Drawings

airplane	fish
angry face	flower
apple	H
ball	happy face
butterfly	hat
cap	heart
car	house
chair	ice-cream cone
church	notebook
circle	ruler
cloud	sad face
comb	square
crown	table
cup	television
door	tree
egg	triangle
envelope	umbrella
eye	window

The page numbers following the symbol > refer to the Look and Say activities, which are in Unit 2.

→ *Unit 1: Key Drawings*

Key Drawings

Practice [> pages 24 and 25]

1. Draw a
   | circle. |
   | square. |
   | triangle. |
   | heart. |
   | flower. |

2. Draw a
   | butterfly. |
   | fish. |
   | happy face. |
   | sad face. |
   | cloud. |

3. Draw a
   | notebook. |
   | ruler. |
   | house. |
   | church. |
   | door. |

4. Draw a
   | cup. |
   | ball. |
   | cap. |
   | hat. |
   | crown. |

→ *Unit 1: Key Drawings*

5. Draw a
   | car.
   | comb.
   | television.
   | tree.
   | window.
   | table.
   | chair.

6. Draw an
   | airplane.
   | eye.
   | angry face.
   | ice-cream cone.
   | umbrella.
   | apple.
   | egg.
   | envelope.
   | H.

Optional longer commands

Draw a **circle** and a **flower**.
Draw a **square**, a **flower**, and a **chair**.

Erase (*after each drawing or after a series of drawings*)

Erase the **heart**.
Now erase the **circle**.
Erase the **flower** and the **square**.

Erase it.
Erase them.
Erase everything.

---
*For more commands with **erase**, see Appendix 2.*

Unit 2

Look and Say activities for the Key Drawings

Unit 2: Look and Say activities for the Key Drawings

Look and Say (1)

Choose a figure and tell your students what to draw.

Use

| Draw a **circle**. |

Look and Say (2)

Choose a figure and tell your students what to draw.

Use

Draw a **hat**.
Draw an **eye**.

Unit 3

Practice with the Key Drawings

The numbers in bold refer to the specific practice activities.

> a/an **1**
>
> adjective before noun *(a big hat)* **2**
>
> big/small **2**
>
> very/fairly *(very big, fairly small)* **2**
>
> tiny/huge **2**
>
> a/some/a few **3, 4**
>
> noun plurals **3, 4**
>
> it/they *(it is/they are)* **3**
>
> it/them **4**
>
> there is/there are **5**
>
> inside **5**

There are no Look and Say activities for this unit.

Unit 3: Practice with the Key Drawings

Practice

1. Draw

a	ball.	notebook.	cap.
	chair.	ruler.	hat.
	fish.	square.	table.
	happy face.	window.	church.
an	apple.	airplane.	
	envelope.	angry face.	
	egg.	umbrella.	
	eye.	ice-cream cone.	

2. Draw a

> big
> small
> fairly big
> fairly small
> very big
> very small
> huge
> tiny

cloud.

cloud	hat	angry face
envelope	airplane	flower
window	ball	notebook
eye	ruler	umbrella
church	sad face	apple

butterfly	car	crown
cap	heart	egg
happy face	television	house
chair	comb	square
circle	door	table

Unit 3: Practice with the Key Drawings

3. Draw

a	circle. cloud. hat. flower. tree.
two some a few	eyes. umbrellas. eggs. notebooks. doors.

■
It's
They're

big.
small.

4. Draw

a	fish. cup. butterfly. sad face. happy face.
two some a few	squares. triangles. windows. chairs. hearts.

■ Make
it
them

big.
small.

29

Unit 3: Practice with the Key Drawings

5. Draw a big | square. / circle. / rectangle.

There's a	flower house ball heart tree	happy face sad face crown fish butterfly	inside it.
There are two	cups eyes hats clouds	chairs windows circles triangles	

Unit 4

In the center − At the top − At the bottom

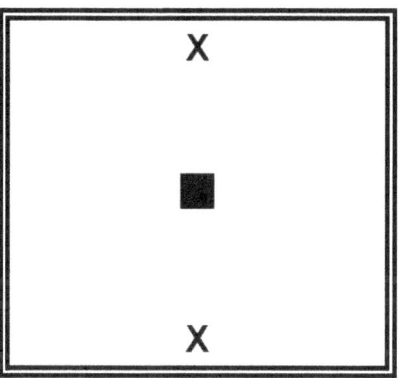

Unit 4: In the center – At the top – At the bottom

In the center – At the top – At the bottom

Presentation

Draw a square.

1. In the center, draw a house.
2. At the top, draw a heart.
3. At the bottom, draw a door.

Practice

Draw a square.

■ | In the center, / At the top, / At the bottom, | draw a* | flower. cap.   apple. / crown. heart.   egg. / house. window. umbrella. / tree.   television. H. / car.   butterfly. eye. / hat.   square.   airplane. / sad face. ball.   envelope.

---

* Before words beginning with a vowel sound use AN: *an egg.*

Unit 4: In the center – At the top – At the bottom

Look and Say

Choose a square and tell your students what to draw.
For each "drawing" the students will need a new square.

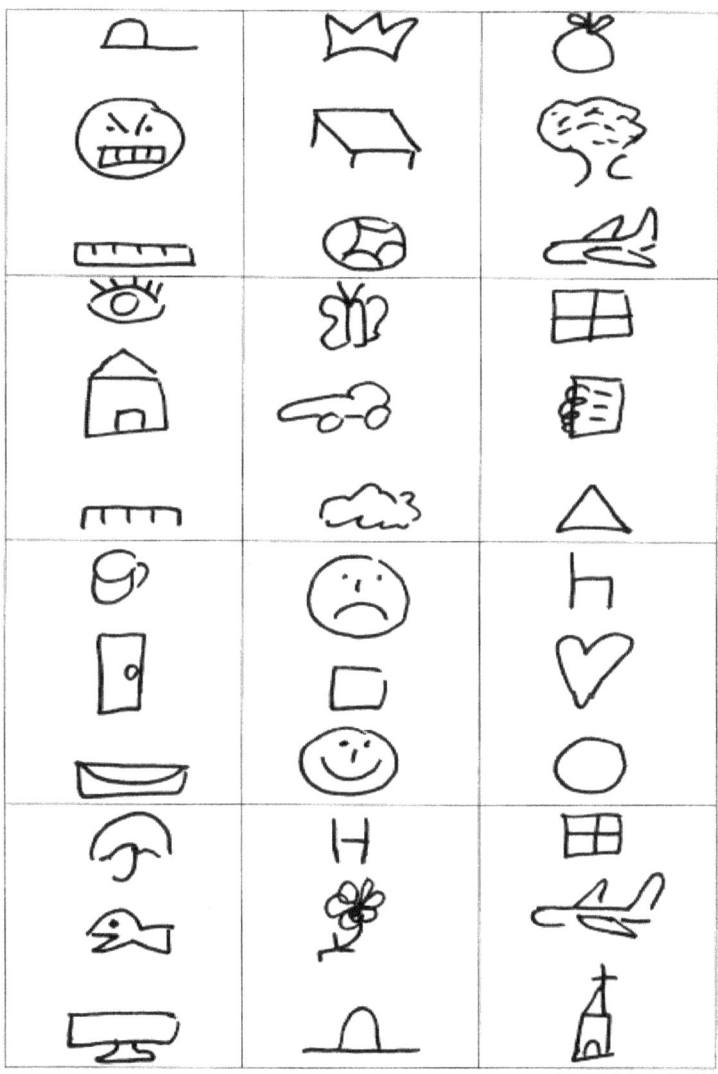

Use

In the center ■ At the top ■ At the bottom

Unit 5

Next to, on the left

Next to, on the right

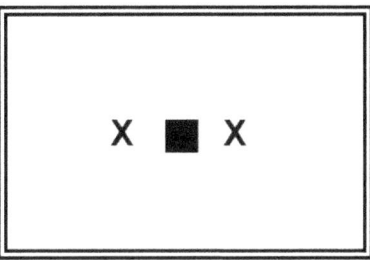

Unit 5: Next to, on the left – Next to on the right

Next to, on the left – Next to, on the right

Presentation

Draw a rectangle.
1. In the center, draw a church.
2. Next to the church, on the left, draw a hat.
3. Next to the church, on the right, draw a chair.

Practice

Draw a rectangle.

1. In the center, draw a **church.**

2. Next to the **church,** on the left, / on the right, draw a **hat.**

flower	cloud	notebook	apple
circle	comb	happy face	egg
triangle	fish	television	ice-cream cone
house	cup	door	angry face
table	ball	butterfly	umbrella

Unit 5: Next to, on the left – Next to on the right

Look and Say

*Choose a rectangle and tell your students what to draw.
For each "drawing" the students will need a new rectangle.*

Use

In the center ■ Next to, on the left ■ Next to, on the right

→ *Unit 6: Five Positions*

 Unit 6

Five Positions

In the center

At the top

At the bottom

Next to, on the left

Next to, on the right

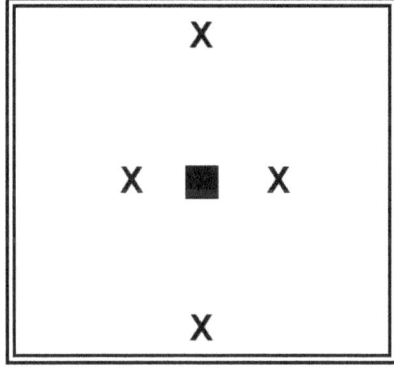

→ Unit 6: Five Positions

In the center – At the top – At the bottom
Next to, on the left – Next to, on the right

Presentation

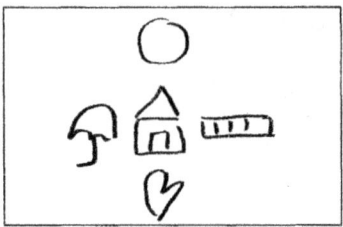

Draw a rectangle.
1. In the center, draw a house.
2. At the top, draw a circle.
3. At the bottom, draw a heart.
4. Next to the house, on the left, draw an umbrella.
5. Next to the house, on the right, draw a ruler.

Practice

Draw a rectangle.

1. In the center,
   At the top,
   At the bottom, | draw a **door**.

2. Next to the **door**, | on the left, on the right, | draw a **ball**.

*

television	cloud	church	airplane
ball	crown	flower	umbrella
butterfly	notebook	table	H
door	triangle	tree	angry face
heart	window	happy face	envelope

* Before words beginning with a vowel sound, use AN: *an egg.*

→ *Unit 6: Five Positions*

Look and Say

*Choose a rectangle and tell your students what to draw.
For each "drawing" the students will need a new rectangle.*

Use

In the center	■ At the top	■ At the bottom
Next to, on the left	■ Next to, on the right	

Unit 7

Over – Under

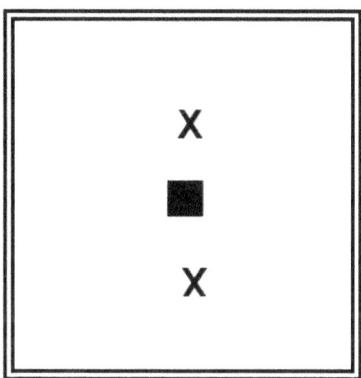

Unit 7: Over – Under

Over – Under

Presentation

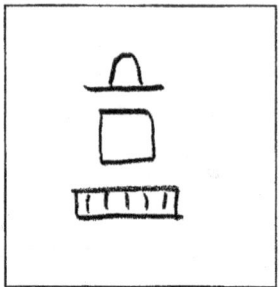

Draw a square.
1. In the center, draw a square.
2. Over the square, draw a hat.
3. Under the square, draw a ruler.

Practice

Draw a square.
1. In the center, draw a **window**.
2. | Over |
   | Under | the **window**, draw a **car**.

*

door	fish	circle	apple
comb	happy face	cup	egg
sad face	house	window	eye
cap	cloud	car	umbrella
ball	chair	heart	airplane

---

* Before words beginning with a vowel sound, use AN: *an egg.*

Unit 7: Over – Under

Look and Say

*Choose a square and tell your students what to draw.
For each "drawing" the students will need a new square.*

Use

In the center
Over ■ Under

Unit 8

Seven Positions

In the center

At the top

At the bottom

Next to, on the left

Next to, on the right

Over

Under

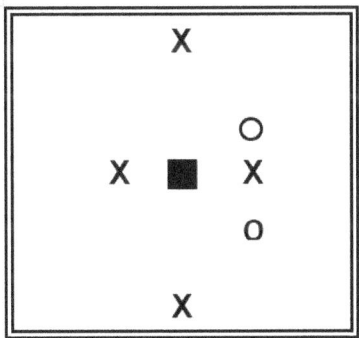

Unit 8: Seven Positions

In the center – At the top – At the bottom
Next to, on the left – Next to, on the right
Over – Under

Presentation

Draw a big rectangle.
1. In the center, draw a tree.
2. At the top, draw a fish.
3. At the bottom, draw an angry face.
4. Next to the tree, on the left, draw a flower.
5. Next to the tree, on the right, draw an envelope.
6. Over the flower, draw a cloud.
7. Under the envelope, draw a triangle.

Practice (1)

Draw a rectangle.

1. | In the center,
 At the top,
 At the bottom, | draw a **comb**.

2. Next to the **comb**, | on the left, <br> on the right, | draw a **car**.

3. | Over
 Under | the **car**, draw a **door**.

*

fish	hat	cap	envelope
sad face	notebook	ball	apple
chair	butterfly	house	egg
ruler	table	television	eye
church	circle	square	umbrella
window	heart	crown	ice-cream cone

Practice (2) *[optional]*

Do Practice (1) again, this time using *THERE'S*.

>In the center, there's a comb.
>At the top, there's a heart.
>Etc.

---

* Before words beginning with a vowel sound, use AN: *an egg.*

49

→ *Unit 8: Seven Positions*

Look and Say

*Choose a rectangle and tell your students what to draw.
For each "drawing" the students will need a new rectangle.*

Use

In the center ■ At the top ■ At the bottom
Next to, on the left ■ Next to, on the right
Over ■ Under

All Four Corners

In the upper left-hand corner
In the upper right-hand corner
In the lower left-hand corner
In the lower right-hand corner

All Four Corners

Presentation

Draw a rectangle.
1. In the upper left-hand corner, draw a circle.
2. In the upper right-hand corner, draw a square.
3. In the lower left-hand corner, draw a triangle.
4. In the lower right-hand corner, draw a heart.

Practice

Draw a rectangle.

- In the | upper / lower | left-hand corner, / right-hand corner, | draw a **circle**.

*

butterfly	door	flower	eye
cloud	ruler	cap	apple
car	tree	chair	umbrella
comb	house	hat	H
ball	television	window	angry face

---

* Before words beginning with a vowel sound, use AN: *an egg*

Unit 9: All Four Corners

Look and Say

*Choose a rectangle and tell your students what to draw.
For each "drawing" the students will need a new rectangle.*

Use

In the upper left-hand corner ■	In the upper right-hand corner
In the lower left-hand corner ■	In the lower right-hand corner

53

Unit 10

Eleven Positions

In the center
At the top
At the bottom

Next to, on the left
Next to, on the right

In the upper left-hand corner
In the upper right-hand corner
In the lower left-hand corner
In the lower right-hand corner

Over
Under

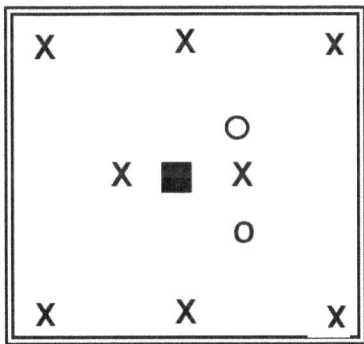

Eleven Positions

Presentation

Draw a big rectangle.

1. In the center, draw a house.
2. At the top, draw an airplane.
3. At the bottom, draw a car.
4. In the upper left-hand corner, draw a circle.
5. In the upper right-hand corner, draw a chair.
6. In the lower left-hand corner, draw a door.
7. In the lower right-hand corner, draw a ball.
8. Next to the house, on the left, draw a ruler.
9. Next to the house, on the right, draw an envelope.
10. Over the envelope, draw a hat.
11. Under the envelope, draw a heart.

Practice (1)

Draw a rectangle.

1. | In the center, / At the top, / At the bottom, | draw a **house**.

2. In the | upper / lower | | left-hand corner, / right-hand corner, | draw a **circle**.

3. Next to the house, | on the left, / on the right, | draw a **ruler**.

4. | Over / Under | the **ruler**, draw a **heart**.

*

table	cap	tree	egg
church	cloud	happy face	ice-cream cone
television	fish	notebook	angry face
butterfly	flower	crown	umbrella
sad face	window	cup	apple
ball	circle	square	envelope
chair	comb	car	eye

Practice (2) *[optional]*

Do Practice (1) again, this time using *THERE'S*.

In the center, there's a house.
In the upper left-hand corner, there's a circle.
Etc.

---

* Before words beginning with a vowel sound, use AN: *an egg*.

➜ *Unit 10: Eleven Positions*

Look and Say

*Choose a rectangle and tell your students what to draw.
For each "drawing" the students will need a new rectangle.*

Drawing 1

Drawing 2

In the center ■ At the top ■ At the bottom
Next to, on the left ■ Next to, on the right
In the upper/lower right-hand corner ■ In the upper/lower left-hand corner
Under ■ Over

→ *Unit 10: Eleven Positions*

Drawing 3

Drawing 4

In the center   ■   At the top   ■   At the bottom
Next to, on the left   ■   Next to, on the right
In the upper/lower right-hand corner   ■   In the upper/lower left-hand corner
Under   ■   Over

Unit 10: Eleven Positions

Drawing 5

Drawing 6

In the center ■ At the top ■ At the bottom
Next to, on the left ■ Next to, on the right
In the upper/lower right-hand corner ■ In the upper/lower left-hand corner
Under ■ Over

→ *Unit 10: Eleven Positions*

Drawing 7

Drawing 8

In the center ■ At the top ■ At the bottom
Next to, on the left ■ Next to, on the right
In the upper/lower right-hand corner ■ In the upper/lower left-hand corner
Under ■ Over

➜ *Unit 10: Eleven Positions*

Drawing 9

Drawing 10

In the center ■ At the top ■ At the bottom
Next to, on the left ■ Next to, on the right
In the upper/lower right-hand corner ■ In the upper/lower left-hand corner
Under ■ Over

Unit 11

Preparatory for Advanced Drawings-1

The numbers in bold refer to the specific practice activities.

upside-down **1**
broken lines **2**

with **2, 7**
between **3, 4**
in front of – in back of *(behind)* **5**
over – under **5, 6**
around **6**
next to *(beside)* **6**
in *(inside)* – on *(on top of)* **6**

vocabulary to describe a face **7**

long hair	a beard
short hair	a long beard
curly hair	a short beard
big ears	a mustache
small eyes	a big mustache
	a long nose
	a big nose

Unit 11: *Preparatory for Advanced Drawings-1*

Practice

> The pages following the symbol > refer to the corresponding Look and Say activities, which are in Unit 12.

1. Draw an upside-down | tree. / airplane. / house. / church. / umbrella. | [> page 68]

2. Draw a | square / rectangle / triangle / heart / circle | with broken lines. [> page 68]

3. Draw a | ruler / flower / butterfly / heart / window | between two | trees. / houses. / churches. / happy faces. / sad faces. |

    [> page 69]

4. Draw a | triangle / circle / comb / crown | between a | chair / ball / cap / cup | and a | table. / cloud. / hat. / car. |

    [> page 69]

Unit 11: Preparatory for Advanced Drawings-1

5. Draw
   - a fish.
   - a car.
   - a bus.
   - an airplane.

   [> page 70]

- ■
  - In front of
  - In back of *(behind)*
  - Under
  - Over

  it, draw a

  - cloud.
  - notebook.
  - window.
  - cap.
  - crown.

> For objects having a definite front and back, always draw them facing left. That way the drawings will always be the same.

6. Draw a
   - square.
   - triangle.
   - rectangle.

   [> page 71]

- ■ Now draw a circle
  - over
  - under
  - next to *(beside)*
  - on *(on top of)*
  - in *(inside)*
  - around

  it.

7. Draw
   - a happy face
   - a sad face
   - an angry face

   with

   - long hair.
   - short hair.
   - curly hair.
   - a beard.
   - a long beard.
   - a mustache.
   - a big mustache.
   - a long nose.
   - a big nose.
   - big ears.
   - small eyes.

   [> page 72]

Unit 12

Look and Say activities for Unit 11

> The numbers following the symbol > refer to the corresponding Practice activities, which are in Unit 11.

Unit 12: Look and Say activities for Unit 11

Look and Say (1) [> page 64 # 1, 2]

Choose a square and tell your students what to draw.

Ex. Draw a square with broken lines.
Draw an upside-down house.

Look and Say (2)   [> page 64 # 3, 4]

Choose a rectangle and tell your students what to draw.

Ex. Draw a butterfly between two eyes.

Ex. Draw an H between a crown and a hat.

Unit 12: Look and Say activities for Unit 11

Look and Say (3) [> page 65 # 5]

Choose a square and tell your students what to draw.
Ex. In the center, draw a fish.
In front of the fish, draw an umbrella.

Use

In the center
In front of ■ In back of *(behind)*
Over ■ Under

Unit 12: Look and Say activities for Unit 11

Look and Say (4)   [> pages 65 # 6]

Choose a square and tell your students what to draw.

Ex. Draw a square.
Now draw a circle over it.

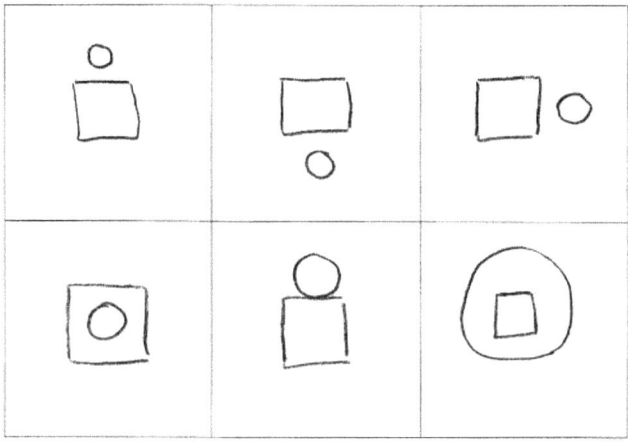

Ex. Draw a triangle.
Now draw a circle over it.

Use

Over ■ Under ■ Around
In *(inside)* ■ Next to *(beside)*
On *(on top of)*

Unit 12: Look and Say activities for Unit 11

Look and Say (5)   [> page 65 # 7]

Choose a square and tell your students what to draw.
Ex. Draw a happy face with long hair and a big nose.

Use

Happy face ■ Sad face ■ Angry face
Long *(short, curly)* hair ■ Long *(short)* beard
Big *(small)* mustache ■ Big *(small)* eyes *(ears)*
Big *(small, long)* nose

Unit 13

Advanced Drawings-1

All eleven positions and vocabulary from Unit 11

> in the center − at the top − at the bottom
> next to, on the left − next to, on the right
> over − under
> in the upper left-hand corner − in the upper right-hand corner
> in the lower left-hand corner − in the lower right-hand corner

in front of	in *(inside)* over
in back of *(behind)*	on *(on top of)* under
next to *(beside)*	around
between	with
upside-down	a beard
broken lines	a long beard
long hair	a short beard
short hair	a mustache
curly hair	a big mustache
big ears	a long nose
small eyes	a big nose

→ *Unit 13: Advanced Drawings-1*

Read and Say (1)

Read and tell your students what to draw.

1. In the center, there's a house.
2. At the top, draw an airplane.
3. At the bottom, there's a car.
4. In the upper left-hand corner, draw a heart.
5. Next to the house, on the left, draw a notebook.
6. In the lower right-hand corner, draw a triangle with broken lines.
7. In back of the airplane, draw a flower.
8. In the lower left-hand corner, draw a door.
9. Beside the house, on the right, there's a happy face with a beard.
10. In the upper right-hand corner, draw a circle.
11. Over the notebook, draw an envelope.
12. Under the circle, draw a tree.
13. In front of the car, draw a sad face with big ears.
14. Between the heart and the door, there's an upside-down church.
15. Behind the car, draw a window.

→ Unit 13: Advanced Drawings-1

Read and Say (2)

Read and tell your students what to draw.

1. In the center, there's a square with a circle inside it.
2. In the lower right-hand corner, draw an apple.
3. At the top, there's a butterfly.
4. In the upper left-hand corner, draw a crown.
5. Under the crown, there are two eyes.
6. In the lower left-hand corner, draw a cup.
7. At the bottom, draw a bus.
8. On top of it, draw a chair.
9. Beside the square, on the left, there's a happy face with a long beard.
10. Next to the square, on the right, draw a fish.
11. In the upper right-hand corner, draw a ball.
12. Behind the fish, draw a small triangle.
13. Now draw two circles around the triangle.
14. In front of the bus, draw an upside-down umbrella.
15. Over the fish, there's a cloud.
16. Under the two circles, draw an angry face with curly hair.

Read and Say (3)

Read and tell your students what to draw.

1. At the top, draw a sad face with short hair and a big mustache.
2. In the center, draw a tree.
3. Beside it, on the left, draw a comb.
4. Under the tree, there's a bird.
5. In the upper left-hand corner, draw a cap.
6. Behind the bird, there's a happy face with long hair and a big nose.
7. In the lower left-hand corner, draw a house with two doors.
8. In the upper right-hand corner, draw a circle in a triangle.
9. In the lower right-hand corner, draw an egg.
10. In front of the bird, draw a window.
11. Between the cap and the sad face, there's a square with broken lines.
12. Over the house, draw a hat.
13. Under the triangle, draw an H.
14. Between the H and the egg, there's a notebook.
15. Next to the sad face, on the right, draw a ruler.

Read and Say (4)

Read and tell your students what to draw.

1. In the center, draw a sad face with curly hair and a long nose.
2. At the bottom, draw an airplane.
3. In front of it, there's an upside-down tree.
4. In the upper left-hand corner, draw a ball.
5. At the top, draw a car.
6. In the upper right-hand corner, draw an ice-cream cone.
7. In the lower left-hand corner, there's an envelope with broken lines.
8. In back of the car, draw a flower.
9. Next to the sad face, on the left, there's a square.
10. In the lower right-hand corner, draw a heart.
11. Between the sad face and the ice-cream cone, draw a butterfly.
12. Beside the square, on the left, draw a comb.
13. Over the heart, draw a small chair.
14. Now draw a circle around the chair.
15. Under the ball, there are three small triangles.

Unit 13: Advanced Drawings-1

Read and Say (5)

Read and tell your students what to draw.

1. At the bottom, draw an angry face with short hair and big ears.
2. In the center, there's a rectangle with three circles in it.
3. On top of it, draw a ball.
4. Next to the rectangle, on the right, there's an umbrella.
5. Draw an egg in the lower left-hand corner.
6. There's a cloud over the umbrella.
7. Draw an apple in the upper left-hand corner.
8. At the top, draw a fish.
9. Draw a church between the egg and the angry face.
10. In the upper right-hand corner, draw an eye.
11. Under the umbrella, draw a ruler.
12. There's a window beside the rectangle, on the left.
13. Draw a small square in back of the fish.
14. There's a heart in front of the fish.
15. In the lower right-hand corner, draw a hat.

→ **Unit 13: Advanced Drawings-1**

Read and Say (6)

Read and tell your students what to draw.

1. In the center, draw a heart.
2. Next to the heart, on the right, there's a happy face with big eyes, small ears, and short hair.
3. There's a car at the bottom.
4. Draw a cup in the lower left-hand corner.
5. Draw a crown in back of the car.
6. In front of the car, draw comb.
7. In the upper left-hand corner, there's a house.
8. Draw a ruler under the heart.
9. In the upper right-hand corner, draw a table.
10. In the lower right-hand corner, draw a window.
11. Beside the heart, on the left, there's a sad face with curly hair and a beard.
12. At the top, draw a chair between two clouds.
13. Over the window, draw a butterfly.
14. Draw a notebook between the table and the butterfly.
15. Between the house and the cup, there's a triangle with a heart in it.

➜ *Unit 13: Advanced Drawings-1*

Read and Say (7)

Read and tell your students what to draw.

1. In the center, there's a happy face with curly hair and a big mustache.
2. At the top, there are three triangles.
3. Draw an upside-down house in the lower left-hand corner.
4. Draw a heart with broken lines in the upper left-hand corner.
5. At the bottom, draw a fish.
6. In back of it, there's a tree.
7. Next to the happy face, on the left, there's a butterfly inside a square.
8. Beside the happy face, on the right, draw a big umbrella.
9. Draw a window on top of the umbrella.
10. There's a chair in the upper right-hand corner.
11. Under the square, draw a ruler.
12. In the lower right-hand corner, draw a church.
13. Draw a circle between the heart and the square.
14. There's a cloud over the church.

→ *Unit 13: Advanced Drawings-1*

Read and Say (8)

Read and tell your students what to draw.

1. In the upper left-hand corner, draw an angry face with short hair and a long beard.
2. Draw an airplane in the center.
3. Behind it, draw a big triangle with a little triangle inside it.
4. In the upper right-hand corner, draw a door.
5. At the top, there's a rectangle with an eye inside it.
6. Draw a ball in the lower left-hand corner.
7. In the lower right-hand corner, draw a sad face with long hair.
8. There's a crown in front of the airplane.
9. Draw an envelope over the ball.
10. At the bottom, draw an apple between two trees.
11. Under the door, there are three circles.
12. Over the sad face in the lower right-hand corner, draw a rectangle with broken lines.

Read and Say (9)

Read and tell your students what to draw.

1. At the top, draw a happy face with curly hair and a long nose.
2. In the center, draw a car.
3. In back of it, there's a house.
4. Draw a notebook in the upper left-hand corner.
5. In the upper right-hand corner, draw an umbrella.
6. In front of the car, draw an upside-down heart with broken lines.
7. There's an airplane at the bottom.
8. Draw a rectangle in the lower left-hand corner.
9. Inside the rectangle, there are two triangles.
10. On top of it, draw a chair.
11. In the lower right-hand corner, there's a sad face with short hair and three eyes.
12. Next to the house, on the right, draw a comb.
13. There's a hat over the comb.
14. Under the notebook, draw a flower.

Unit 13: Advanced Drawings-1

Read and Say (10)

Read and tell your students what to draw.

1. At the bottom, there's a sad face with short hair and a big nose.
2. Draw a triangle in the lower left-hand corner.
3. At the top, draw an upside-down tree.
4. In the upper right-hand corner, there's an ice-cream cone.
5. Draw a fish in the center.
6. In the upper left-hand corner, draw a comb.
7. In the lower right-hand corner, there's a heart.
8. There's a butterfly under the comb.
9. Behind the fish, draw a ruler.
10. In front of the fish, draw a square.
11. Draw an eye on top of the square.
12. Over the heart, draw a cloud.
13. Beside the sad face, on the right, draw a hat.
14. There's a church between the sad face and the triangle.

Unit 14

The numbers in bold refer to the specific practice activities.

>horizontal line **1**
>vertical line **1**
>diagonal line **1**
>curved line **1**
>wavy line **1**
>
>long – short **2**
>
>ordinal numbers **7**
>
>star **1**
>diamond **1**
>dollar sign **1**
>pound sign *(hashtag symbol)* **1**
>question mark **1**

>a few **2**
>some **2**
>a lot of **2**
>lots of **2**
>
>between **2**
>inside **3**
>on top of **3**
>beside **3**
>over **3, 4**
>under **3, 4**
>around **6**
>of **6**
>
>big one – small one **3**
>big ones – small ones **4**
>
>one – the other – both **5**
>the first one – the others **6**

85

Unit 14: Preparatory for Advanced Drawings-2

Practice

> The pages following the symbol > refer to the corresponding Look and Say activities, which are in Unit 15.

1. Draw a
   - horizontal line.
   - vertical line.
   - diagonal line.
   - curved line.
   - wavy line
   - star.
   - diamond.
   - dollar sign.
   - pound sign *(hashtag symbol)*
   - question mark.

2. Draw
   - a few
   - some
   - a lot of
   - lots of

   - Xs
   - Bs
   - triangles
   - squares
   - circles
   - hearts
   - clouds
   - stars
   - crowns
   - chairs
   - diamonds

   between two

   - vertical lines.
   - horizontal lines
   - diagonal lines.
   - curved lines.

   [> page 92]

   You can increase the difficulty by using:
   between two **broken** vertical lines
   between two **long/short** vertical lines
   between two **long/short broken** vertical lines

Unit 14: Preparatory for Advanced Drawings-2

3. Draw a big | circle / rectangle / square | and a small one.   [> page 93]

- Draw a | star / triangle / heart / flower / ball / hat / fish / chair / door / crown / cloud | inside / on top of / over / under / beside | the | big / small | one.

4. Draw two big | circles / rectangles / squares | and two small ones.

[> page 94]

- Draw a | horizontal line / curved line / wavy line | over / under | the | big / small | ones.

> You could also have your students draw more than one line: *Draw two wavy lines over the big ones.*

Unit 14: Preparatory for Advanced Drawings-2

5. Draw two
   | eyes.
   | flowers.
   | notebooks.
   | umbrellas.
   | houses.
   | churches.
   | envelopes.
   | crowns.
   | clouds.
   | trees.
   | hats.

   [> page 95]

- One is big, and the other is small.

   or

- Both are big.

   or

- Both are small.

6. Draw a row of four
   | hearts.
   | chairs.
   | cups.
   | Bs.
   | balls.
   | triangles.

- Draw a circle *(square)* around the first one and a rectangle around the others.

Unit 14: Preparatory for Advanced Drawings-2

7. Draw a row of six big squares. [> page 96]
   Number them, putting a number above each square.

- Draw a | B / star / heart / triangle / circle / window | in the | first / second / third / fourth / fifth / last | square.

More things to draw in the squares

flower	tree	ball
cloud	comb	butterfly
cup	table	television
chair	hat	eye *(an)*
square	house	umbrella *(an)*
fish	crown	apple *(an)*

Don't give the commands in order beginning with the first square. Vary the order. Continue until you have placed an object in each square.

Unit 15

Look and Say activities for Unit 14

The numbers following the symbol > refer to the corresponding Practice activities, which are in Unit 14.

Unit 15: Look and Say activities for Unit 14

Look and Say (1)   [> page 86 #2]

Choose a square and tell your students what to draw.
Ex. Draw some stars between two horizontal lines.

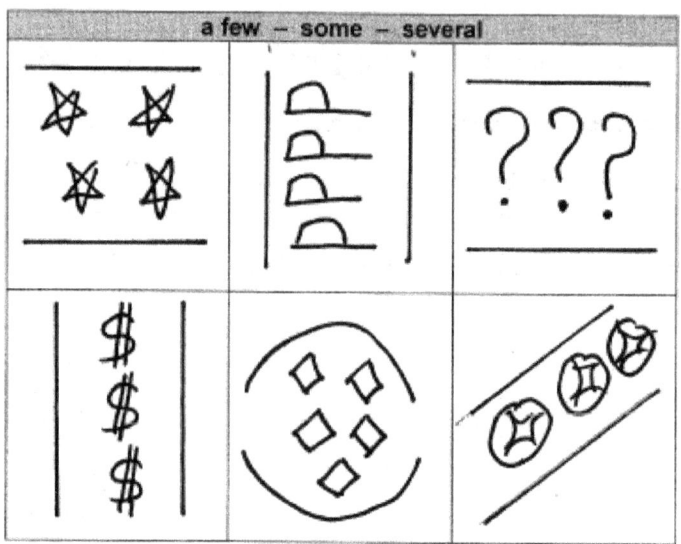

Ex. Draw a lot of hearts between two vertical lines.

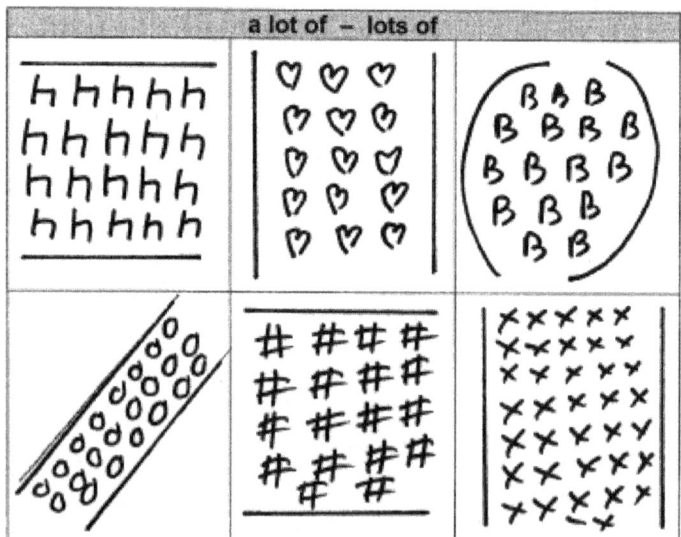

Unit 15: Look and Say activities for Unit 14

Look and Say (2) [> page 87 #3]

Choose a square and tell your students what to draw.
    Ex. Draw a big circle and a small one.
- Draw a star inside the small one.
- Now draw an airplane over the big one.

Use

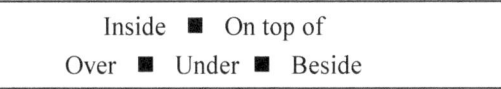

Unit 15: Look and Say activities for Unit 14

Look and Say (3) [> page 87 #4]

Choose a square and tell your students what to draw.

Ex. Draw two big circles and two small ones.
- Draw a wavy line over the big ones.
- Now draw a horizontal line over the small ones.

Use

| Over ■ Under |

Unit 15: Look and Say activities for Unit 14

Look and Say (4) [> page 88 #5]

Choose a square and tell your students what to draw.

Ex. Draw two circles.
- One is big, and the other is small.

One is / the other is   **Both are big.**   **Both are small.**

Use

One is big, and the other is small.
Both are big. ■ Both are small.

95

Unit 15: Look and Say activities for Unit 14

Look and Say (5) [> page 89 #7]

Choose a row and tell your students what to draw.

Ex. Draw a row of five big squares and number them.
- Draw a hat in the fourth square.
- Draw a question mark in the second square.

Unit 16

The numbers in bold refer to the specific practice activities.

has **1, 4, 5, 6, 7**
for **1**
its *(It has stars for its eyes.)* **1**
doesn't have **1**
any *(doesn't have any hair)* **1**
a little *(a little bigger)* **2**
a lot *(a lot bigger)* **2**
much *(much bigger)* **2**
comparatives with –ER **2**
superlatives with –EST **3**
foot – feet **4**
ING phrases *(the man wearing a hat)* **4, 5**
present progressive *(He's wearing a hat.)* **6, 7**

♦

hat	dress	glasses	hair
cap	skirt	sunglasses	ear
tie	blouse	earrings	eye
bow tie	necklace	shorts	nose
T-shirt		boots	mouth

♦Clothing vocabulary items are in activities **4** and **5**. Vocabulary items for parts of the face are in activities **1, 4,** and **5**.

Unit 16: Preparatory for Advanced Drawings-2

Practice

> The pages following the symbol > refer to the corresponding Look and Say activities, which are in Unit 17.

1. Draw a face. [> page 102]

   1. It has | hearts / stars / question marks / dollar signs | for its eyes.

   2. It has | hearts / squares / rectangles | for its ears.

   3. It has a | circle / square / triangle / heart | for its nose.

   4. It has a | circle / rectangle / triangle | for its mouth.

   5. It has | short / curly | hair.

       or

       It doesn't have any hair.

Unit 16: Preparatory for Advanced Drawings-2

2. Draw a **circle** and a **square**.   [> page 103]

   - The **circle** is [**bigger** / **smaller**] than the **square**.

circle	fish	hat
square	door	heart
triangle	window	house
chair	comb	happy face
cloud	tree	sad face

   > You can also use:
   > **a little** bigger; **a lot** smaller; **much** bigger

3. Draw three **hearts** in a row.   [> page 104]

   - The **heart** [on the right / on the left / in the middle] is [the biggest. / the smallest.]

circles	trees	flowers
squares	crowns	houses
triangles	windows	happy faces
chairs	combs	sad faces
clouds	stars	angry faces
balls	eyes	umbrellas
hearts	hats	question marks

Unit 16: Preparatory for Advanced Drawings-2

With participial phrases   [> pages 105 and 106]

4. Draw a man wearing

| a hat. a cap. a tie. a bow tie. a T-shirt. | glasses. sunglasses. shorts. |

- He has

| long hair *(short hair, curly hair).* big ears. one big ear and one small one. big feet. one big foot and one small one. |

5. Draw a woman wearing

| a dress. a skirt. blouse. a hat. a necklace. | boots. earrings. glasses. sunglasses. shorts. |

- She has

| long hair *(short hair, curly hair).* big ears. one big ear and one small one. big hands. one big hand and one small one. |

With the present progressive   [> page 106]

6. Draw a man.
   - He's wearing _____.
   - He has _____.

7. Draw a woman.
   - She's wearing _____.
   - She has _____.

Unit 17

Look and Say activities for Unit 16

The numbers following the symbol > refer to the corresponding Practice activities, which are in Unit 16.

Unit 17: Look and Say activities for Unit 16

Look and Say (1)   [> page 98 #1]

Choose a square and tell your students what to draw.

Ex. Draw a face. It has hearts for its eyes, squares for its ears, a circle for its nose, and a rectangle for its mouth. It doesn't have any hair.

Look and Say (2)   [> page 99 #2]

Choose a rectangle and tell your students what to draw.
    Ex. Draw a circle and a square.
- The circle is bigger than the square.

        or
- The square is smaller than the circle.

Unit 17: Look and Say activities for Unit 16

Look and Say (3) [> page 99 #3]

Choose a rectangle and tell your students what to draw.

Ex. Draw three hearts in a row.
- The heart on the left is the biggest.
  or
- The biggest heart is on the left.

Look and Say (4)   [> page 100 #4 and 5]

Choose a figure and tell your students what to draw.

KEY

Figure 1.
> Draw a man wearing a hat, a tie, and glasses.
> - He has small ears and big feet.

Figure 2.
> Draw a man wearing a cap, a T-shirt, sunglasses, and shorts.
> - He has one big ear and one small one.

Figure 3.
> Draw a man wearing a big bow tie.
> - He has short hair, big ears, and small feet.

Figure 4.
> Draw a woman wearing a dress, a necklace, and earrings.
> - She has curly hair.
> - She has one big foot and one small one.

Figure 5.
> Draw a woman wearing a blouse, a skirt, and boots.
> - She has long hair.
> - She has one big hand and one small one.

Unit 17: Look and Say activities for Unit 16

Look and Say (5)   [> page 100 #4 and 5]

Choose a square and tell your students what to draw.

With ING phrases
    Draw a man wearing a hat, a tie, and sunglasses.
- He has long hair, a small mouth, and small feet.

With the present progressive   [> page 100 #6 and 7]
    Draw a man. *(a woman)*
- He's wearing ____. / She's wearing ____.
- He has ____. / She has ____.

> See Key on next page.

Key to Look and Say (5)

Figure 1
He's wearing a hat, sunglasses, and a tie.
He has long hair, and small feet.

Figure 2
He's wearing a hat, glasses, and a big bow tie.
He has small ears and big feet.

Figure 3
He's wearing a cap, a T-shirt, and shorts.
He has big ears, big eyes, big hands, and small feet.

Figure 4
He's wearing sunglasses, shorts, and a tie.
He has short hair, big ears, and small feet.

Figure 5
He's wearing a crown and a big bow tie.
He has long hair and big feet.

Figure 6
She's wearing a dress, a necklace, and earrings.
She has curly hair, small hands, and small feet.

Figure 7
She's wearing a hat, a dress, sunglasses, earrings, and boots.
She has big hands.

Figure 8
She's wearing glasses, a blouse, and a skirt.
She has curly hair and big feet.
She has one big ear and one small one.

Figure 9
She's wearing a blouse, a skirt, and boots.
She has long hair, and small hands.

Advanced Drawings-2

Structures and vocabulary from units 11, 14, and 16

quantifiers *(a few, some, a lot of)*	with *(with broken lines)*
ordinal numbers *(first, second)*	between
one/ones	around *(around it)*
the other/the others – both	next to *(beside)*
has *(has a circle for its nose)*	in *(inside)*
doesn't have *(doesn't have any ears)*	on *(on top of)*
comparatives with -ER	
superlatives with -EST	
ING phrases *(a fish wearing a hat)*	
present progressive *(He's crying.)*	

horizontal line	upside-down	beard
vertical line	big *(nose, ears)*	mustache
diagonal line	short *(hair, beard)*	eye
curved line	long *(hair, beard, nose)*	ear
wavy line	curly *(hair)*	nose
		mouth
diamond	bow tie	foot
star	tie	feet
dollar sign	sunglasses	man
pound sign	dress	woman
question mark	necklace	

Unit 18: Advanced Drawings-2

New Vocabulary by Drawing*

1	2		3	
any *(any ears)*	animal	name	balloon	only
arrow	cat	put	closest	standing
facing	crying	tall	girl	sun
from ... to	drew	that	holding	tooth
halfway	edge	thin	leg	
It's raining.	extend	this		
pointing	man	write		

4	5		6	7
but	each		each one	fat man
girl	forehead		himself	her
now	head		laughing	herself
teeth	its		leave	his
than	only		space	pocket
through	row			same thing
without	smiling			
	which *(which is)*			
	woman			

8	9	10
also	across	no *(no hair)*
letter	flying a kite	
middle	look at	
not	then	
object	too	

a girl

---

* The chart shows **the first drawing** in which the word is used: it may be used again in other drawings. A few of these words appeared in previous units but received little or no focus.

Unit 18: Advanced Drawings-2

Read and Say (1)
Read and tell your students what to draw.

1. In the center draw a sad face with short hair, a big mustache and hearts for its eyes. It doesn't have any ears.
2. At the top, draw an airplane facing left.
3. In the upper left-hand corner, there's a ball.
4. Draw a broken curved line from the lower right-hand corner to the upper right-hand corner.
5. In the lower left-hand corner, draw a house. It has two doors and three windows.
6. Over the house, there's a cloud, and it's raining.
7. At the bottom, draw an eye.
8. Under the sad face, draw a lot of small circles between two horizontal lines.
9. In front of the airplane, there are two triangles.
10. In back of the airplane, draw an upside-down tree.
11. Next to the sad face, on the left, there's a rectangle with a star inside it.
12. Beside the sad face, on the right, draw a heart.
13. Halfway between the eye and the lower right-hand corner, draw a church.
14. There's an arrow pointing to the ball.

Unit 18: Advanced Drawings-2

Read and Say (2)

Read and tell your students what to draw.

1. In the center, there's a happy face with long hair and big eyes. It has a triangle for its nose.
2. In the lower left-hand corner, there's a fish with a door on its head.
3. In the upper right-hand corner, draw an envelope.
4. Next to the happy face, on the right, draw a tall thin man wearing a crown and a big bow tie. He's crying, and he has big feet.
5. Beside the happy face, on the left, there are three long broken horizontal lines. They extend to the left edge of the rectangle.
6. Over the happy face, draw a ruler.
7. At the bottom draw a cat. This cat has three ears.
8. In the lower right-hand corner, draw a fairly big square.
9. Inside it, write the name of the animal that you drew at the bottom.
10. Under the envelope, there's a long vertical line between two short ones.
11. In the upper left-hand corner, draw a fairly big circle.
12. Now put a dollar sign in it.

Unit 18: Advanced Drawings-2

Read and Say (3)

Read and tell your students what to draw.

1. In the center, draw a tree.
2. At the top, there's a fish wearing a crown.
3. In the lower left-hand corner, draw a chair.
4. Now draw a girl standing on the chair. She has long legs. She's holding an umbrella in one hand and a balloon in the other. The umbrella is in the hand that is closest to the tree.
5. Next to the tree, on the right, draw a rectangle.
6. On top of this rectangle, draw a happy face. It has curly hair, and both ears are big. It has a circle for its nose and triangles for its eyes. There is only one tooth in its mouth.
7. In the lower right-hand corner, draw a notebook.
8. At the bottom, draw four long broken vertical lines between two rectangles.
9. Over the umbrella, draw a butterfly.
10. In the upper right-hand corner, draw the sun.
11. In the upper left-hand corner, draw a pound sign with two circles around it.
12. Under the rectangle, draw a big comb.
13. Behind the fish, draw an eye.

Unit 18: Advanced Drawings-2

Read and Say (4)

Read and tell your students what to draw.

1. In the center, draw an airplane.
2. In front of it, there's a happy face with long hair. It has a long nose, and there are two teeth in its mouth.
3. Under the airplane, draw a girl. She has one big foot and one small one. She's holding a fish in both hands.
4. At the top, draw a triangle and a heart. The triangle is smaller than the heart.
5. Behind the airplane, draw a few stars inside big square.
6. In the lower left-hand corner, draw an egg.
7. In the upper right-hand corner, draw a sad face with curly hair but without a nose. It has one big ear and one small one.
8. In the lower right-hand corner, there's a triangle with broken lines.
9. Draw three diagonal lines from the egg to the happy face.
10. In the upper left-hand corner, draw an upside-down house.
11. Over the triangle that's in the lower right-hand corner, there's an apple.
12. Now draw an arrow through it.
13. Under the square, draw a row of five question marks.

Unit 18: Advanced Drawings-2

Read and Say (5)

Read and tell your students what to draw.

1. In the center, draw a house with two doors.
2. At the top, there are two triangles. The triangle on the right is bigger than the one on the left.
3. Next to the house, on the right, there's an angry face with short hair and a long beard. It doesn't have a nose. It has only one ear, which is small, and there's a heart on its forehead.
4. Draw a cup in the lower left-hand corner.
5. Beside it, draw a woman. She has curly hair. She's wearing sunglasses and big earrings, and she's smiling.
6. Draw a window in the lower right-hand corner. This window is between two broken vertical lines.
7. At the bottom, draw a row of five fairly big squares.
8. Put a dollar sign in each square.
9. Draw an envelope in the upper left-hand corner.
10. Draw a wavy line from the envelope to the woman's head.
11. Next to the house, on the left, there's a ruler.
12. There's a butterfly in the upper right-hand corner.
13. Under this butterfly, draw a flower.
14. Now draw a circle around the flower.

Unit 18: Advanced Drawings-2

Read and Say (6)

Read and tell your students what to draw.

1. In the center, draw a sad face wearing a hat. It has small ears, a short beard, and a triangle for its nose. It has only one eye.
2. Draw an arrow through the hat.
3. There's a car at the bottom.
4. Now draw a man in front of the car. He has short hair and big eyes. He's laughing and pointing to himself.
5. Beside the sad face, on the right, draw a row of five hearts. Leave some space between each one.
6. Draw a circle around the first one and a rectangle around the others.
7. There's a church behind the car.
8. In the upper left-hand corner, draw a cloud inside a square.
9. In the lower right-hand corner, draw a fish with long legs standing on a chair.
10. Over the rectangle that's around the hearts, draw an eye between two vertical lines.
11. Draw a broken diagonal line from the square that's in the upper left-hand corner to the car.

Unit 18: Advanced Drawings-2

Read and Say (7)

Read and tell your students what to draw.

1. There are three triangles at the top. The biggest is on the left, and the smallest is on the right.
2. Draw a square under the biggest triangle and draw a circle around the smallest.
3. In the center, draw a fat man wearing a tie. His hair is short, his ears are small, and his feet are big. There's a big flower in his pocket.
4. Next to the fat man, on the right, draw a row of four fairly big squares.
5. Draw an eye in the second square, and draw a chair in the third one.
6. Put a star in the first square and a hat in the last one.
7. There's a tall woman in the lower left-hand corner. She's wearing a dress, sunglasses, and a necklace. Her hair is curly, her ears are big, her legs are long, and her feet are small. With one hand she's holding an umbrella over her head, and with the other, she's pointing to herself.
8. Under the four squares, draw lots of small circles between two long horizontal lines.
9. Draw four hearts. Put one in the upper left-hand corner, and put the others in the lower right-hand corner.
10. In the upper right hand corner, draw the same thing that you put in the first square but make it bigger.

Unit 18: Advanced Drawings-2

Read and Say (8)

Read and tell your students what to draw.

1. There are three squares at the bottom. The square in the middle is the biggest. The square on the left is smaller than the square on the right.
2. In the center, draw a car. This car is facing left.
3. In back of it, there's an angry face without a nose. It has three ears, one big one and two small ones. Also, it has short curly hair and a long beard.
4. In front of the car, draw an upside-down girl.
5. At the top, there's a butterfly between two curved lines.
6. Draw an ice-cream cone in the upper right-hand corner.
7. In the upper left-hand corner, draw the sun.
8. Put the letter B in the square that's not the biggest and not the smallest.
9. Put a dollar sign in the biggest square.
10. Now put a pound sign in the smallest.
11. Draw a comb in the lower left-hand corner.
12. Over the comb, there are two apples.
13. Draw a heart on top of the biggest square.
14. Now draw an arrow through this heart.
15. Draw a ruler under the object that's in the upper left-hand corner.
16. In the lower right-hand corner, there's a diamond in a circle.

Unit 18: Advanced Drawings-2

Read and Say (9)

Read and tell your students what to draw

1. In the center, draw an envelope.
2. Draw the sun at the top.
3. Now draw a church in the lower left-hand corner.
4. In the lower right-hand corner, draw a table.
5. Between the church and the table, across the bottom, there are five fairly big squares.
6. Next to the envelope, on the left, there's a fat man with a big head, wearing a bow tie. His hair is curly. His nose is big, and his ears are big, too, but his eyes are small. His feet are also small.
7. Beside the envelope, on the right, draw a woman. Her hair is curly. Her ears are small, but her eyes are big. Her feet are also big. She's crying, and she's flying a kite.
8. Over her head, there's a small cloud, and it's raining.
9. Under the envelope, draw a few small triangles inside a circle.
10. Now look at the five squares at the bottom. In the third square, put a dollar sign.
11. In the second, there's a pound sign.
12. Put the letter B inside the fourth square, and then draw an eye on top of it.
13. Draw a happy face in the first square and a sad face in the last one.

Unit 18: Advanced Drawings-2

Read and Say (10)

Read and tell your students what to draw.

1. In the center, there's a heart. It has eyes, a nose, a big mustache, and a circle for its mouth.
2. Draw two big circles and two small ones. Draw the big ones at the top and the small ones at the bottom.
3. Put a star in one of the big circles and a fish in the other.
4. Draw an arrow through both small circles.
5. In the lower left-hand corner, draw a girl standing on a big square. In her hand she's holding an angry face that has one big ear and no hair.
6. This angry face is wearing a crown.
7. Inside the square, there are two question marks.
8. Next to the heart, on the right, draw a big happy face with small ears and a square for its nose. It's wearing sunglasses and a small hat.
9. There's an airplane under this happy face.
10. Behind the airplane, draw a flower.
11. Draw a broken vertical line between the heart and the happy face.
12. There's a ball in the upper right-hand corner.
13. Draw two wavy lines from the upper left-hand corner to the circle at the top.

Appendices

Appendix 1: More Things to Draw

combing	*counting*	*dancing*
drinking	*eating*	*kicking*
pushing	*running*	*singing*
smiling	*thinking*	*walking*

Appendix 1: More Things to Draw

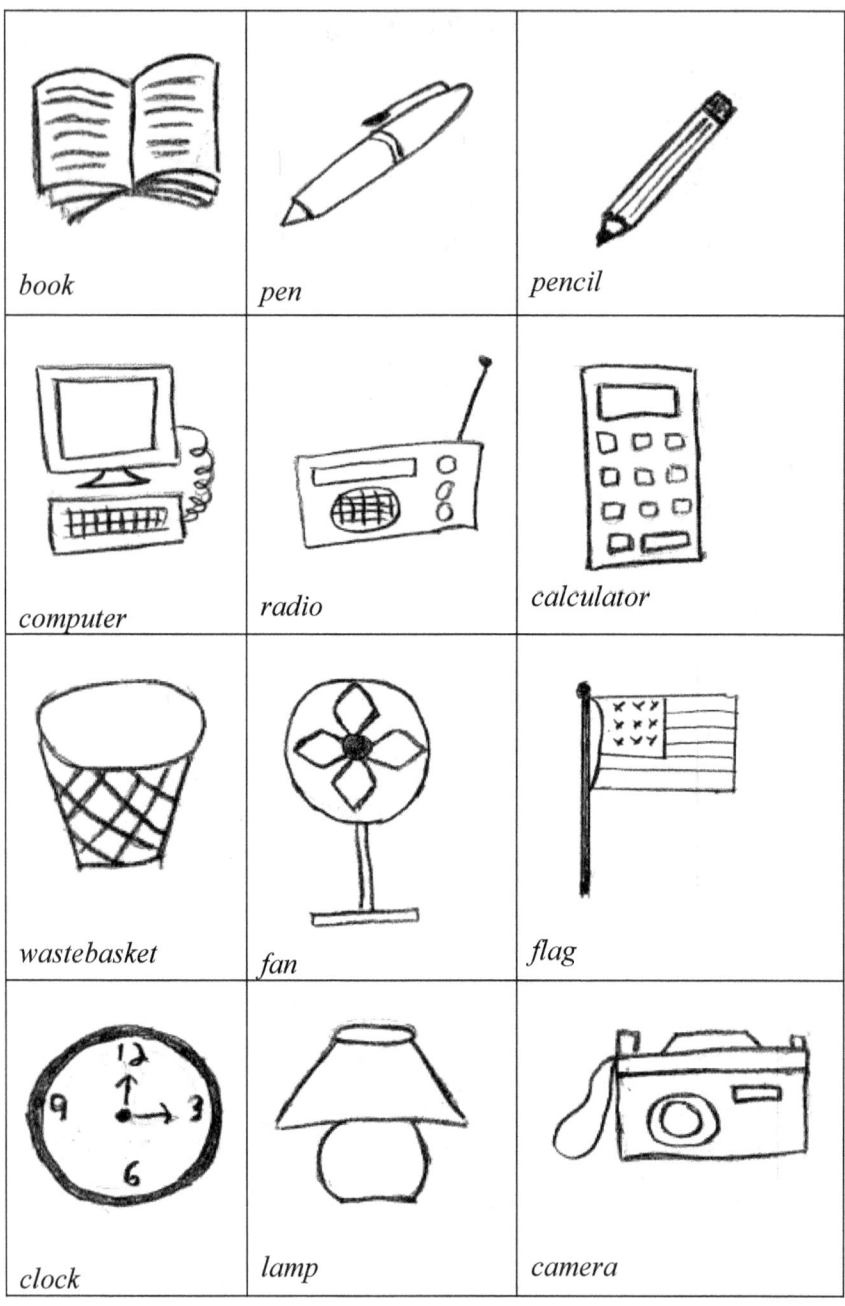

Appendix 1: More Things to Draw

Appendix 2: Erase

Examples of commands with **erase**

1. **Now**
   Now erase it.
   Now erase the flower.

2. **Quickly/slowly**
   Erase it quickly.
   Erase the chair slowly.

3. **And**
   Erase the flower and the chair.

4. **Or**
   Erase the flower or the chair. You decide.

5. **But don't erase** *(Only two items are on the board.)*
   Erase the flower, but don't erase the chair.

6. **Anything else**
   Erase the flower, but don't erase anything else.

7. **Everything**
   Erase everything.
   Erase everything on the board.

8. **That is** *(at, in, on, under, etc.)*
   Erase the object *(drawing)* that's at the top.

9. **Something that's not** *(at, in, on, under, etc.)*
   Erase something that's not at the top.

10. **Which is** *(at, in, on, under, etc.)*
    Erase the object which is at the top.

11. **After/before**
    After you erase the flower, erase the chair.
    Before you erase the circle, erase the church.

12. **After that / before that**
    Erase the flower. After that, erase the chair.
    Erase the flower. Before that, erase the chair.

13. **First … Then**
    First erase the flower. Then erase the chair.

Appendix 3: Practice Some More

Here are some language practice activities you can use with the drawings.

1. **True/False statements**

    T: This is a triangle. *(pointing to a drawing on the board)*
    C: That's true. / That's false.

    T: The triangle is at the top.
    C: That's true. / That's false.

    T: There's a triangle at the top.
    C: That's true. / That's false.

2. **Questions and Answers**

    Yes/No questions

    T: Is this a triangle? *(pointing to a drawing on the board)*
    C: Yes, it is. / No, it isn't.

    T: Is the triangle at the top?
    C: Yes, it is. / No, it isn't.

    T: Is there a triangle at the top?
    C: Yes, there is. / No, there isn't.

    Wh- questions

    T: What's this? *(pointing to a drawing on the board)*
    C: A triangle. It's a triangle.

    T: What's at the top?
    C: The triangle. The triangle is at the top.
    A triangle. There's a triangle at the top.

    T: Where's the triangle?
    C: At the top. It's at the top.

Appendix 3: Practice Some More

3. **Describe the picture**

   There's a heart at the top.
   There's a house in the center.
   There's a door at the bottom

   Or

   There's a heart at the top, a house in the center, and a door at the bottom.

4. **Memory game**

   You erase the board, and the class has to remember what was on it. You can do this after ten to fifteen things have been drawn.

   There was a triangle.
   There were two hearts.
   There was a happy face with long hair.

   You can also erase the objects that have been drawn inside a rectangle, and the class has to reconstruct the original drawing. One student is at the board as the drawer.

   Pedro: In the center, there was a tree.
   (Drawer draws a tree in the center of the rectangle.)

   Maria: At the top, there was a house.
   (Drawer draws a house at the top.)

Appendix 4: Pairwork Language

Drawer language *(spoken to the speaker)*

That's too fast.
You're speaking too fast.
Please speak slower.

I didn't understand.
What did you say?
Could you say that again?
Could you repeat that?
Please repeat that.
Please say that again.

What did you say to draw?
Where did you say to draw the butterfly?
Where does the butterfly go?

Did you say *at the top* or *at the bottom?*

Is this right?
Is this OK?
What do you think of my drawing?

Speaker language *(spoken to the drawer)*

That's too small.
You need to make it bigger.
That's too big.
You need to make it smaller.

Draw it facing left, not facing right.
Draw it at the top, not at the bottom.

Draw it a little more to the left.
Draw it a little more to the right.
Draw it up a little.
Draw it down a little.

Wait. Don't draw yet.
I'm going to say it again.

Are you ready to begin?
Do you want me to speak fast, slow, or normal?

What's this?
Is that really a butterfly?
That's a nice *(fantastic, interesting, strange, crazy)* butterfly.

Appendix 5: Nouns

Appendix 5: Nouns

The numbers in bold refer to the unit where the noun is first used.

Units 1 11 13 14 16		Units 18
airplane **1**	hair **11**	animal
angry face **1**	hand **16**	arrow
apple **1**	happy face **1**	balloon
ball **1**	hashtag symbol **14**	cat
beard **11**	hat **1**	edge
bird **13**	horizontal line **14**	fat man
blouse **16**	house **1**	forehead
boots **16**	ice-cream cone **1**	girl
bow tie **16**	man **16**	head
bus **11**	middle **16**	kite
butterfly **1**	mouth **16**	leg
cap **1**	mustache **11**	letter
car **1**	necklace **16**	man
chair **1**	nose **11**	middle
church **1**	notebook **1**	name
cloud **1**	pound sign **14**	object
comb **1**	question mark **14**	pocket
crown **1**	row **15**	space
cup **1**	ruler **1**	sun
curved line **14**	sad face **1**	teeth
diagonal line **14**	shorts **16**	tooth
diamond **14**	skirt **16**	woman
dollar sign **14**	square **1**	
door **1**	star **14**	
dress **16**	sunglasses **16**	
ear **11**	table **1**	
earrings **16**	television **1**	
egg **1**	tie **16**	
envelope **1**	tree **1**	
eye **1**	triangle **1**	
feet **16**	umbrella **1**	
fish **1**	vertical line **14**	
flower **1**	wavy line **14**	
foot **16**	window **1**	
glasses **16**	woman **16**	

Index of Structures

The numbers after each entry do not refer to pages; they refer to the **unit** where the item first appears or where it receives special focus. Please note that grammatical items in Unit 18 do not receive any special focus; they just occur in one or more of the drawings. Several grammatical items are found in Appendix 2, *Erase* (**A-2**), page 126. These structures can easily be incorporated into any lesson right from the very first unit. There are suggestions for working with Questions and Answers in Appendix 3 (**A-3**), page 127.

Adjectives
    before singular count nouns *(a big circle)* **3, 11**
    before plural count nouns *(big ears)* **11**
    after *be* (*It's big.*) **3**

Adjective clauses (*Erase the object that/which is at the top.*)
    that clauses **A-2, 18**
    which clauses **A-2, 18**

Adverbs
    very (*very big*) **3**
    fairly (*fairly big*) **3**
    a little (*a little bigger*) **16**
    a lot (*a lot bigger*) **16**
    much (*much bigger*) **16**
    quickly **A-2**
    slowly **A-2**
    too **18**
    also **18**
    halfway **18**
    not **A-2, 18**
    now **A-2, 1**
    only (*only one tooth*) **18**
    then **A-2, 18**

Adverb clauses
    after you ... **A-2**
    before you ... **A-2**

Index of structures

Articles
   a 1
   an 1
   a/an 3
   a/some 3
   the (Erase the heart.) 1

Be
   full verb
      is (It's big.) 3
      are (They're big.) 3
   auxiliary verb
      is (is wearing) 16

Comparisons
   comparatives with *–er* 16
   superlatives with *–est* 16
   comparatives with *than* 16

Conjunctions
   and 1
   but **A-2**, 18
   or **A-2**

Demonstrative adjectives
   this (this cat) 18

Do
   doesn't (doesn't have) 16
   don't (negative imperative) **A-2**

Have
   has 16
   have (doesn't have) 16

Imperatives
   affirmative 1
   negative **A-2**

ING phrases *(wearing a hat)* 16

Nouns
   regular plurals 3
   irregular plurals
      feet 16
      teeth 18

Index of Structures

Ordinal numbers 14

Possessive adjectives
her 18
his 18
its (circles for its eyes) 16

Possessive case
's (the woman's head) 18

Prepositions
across 18
after (after that) **A-2**
around (= surrounding/encircling) 11, 14
at (at the top) 4
before (before that) **A-2**
behind 11
beside 11
between 11
for (for its eyes) 16
from ... to 18

in (in the center) 4
in (= inside) 11

in back of 11
in front of 11
inside 11
next to 5
of (a row of) 14

on (on the right) 5
on (= on the upper surface) 11
on (on its forehead) 18
on top of 11

over 7
through 18
under 7
with (= having) 11
without 18

Present progressive 16

133

Index of structures

Pronouns
   subject
      he **16**
      she **16**
      it **3**
      they **3**
   object
      it **3**
      them **3**
   indefinite
      anything (anything else) **A-2**
      everything **A-2**
      something **A-2**
   reflexive
      herself **18**
      himself **18**
   relative
      that **A-2, 18**
      which **A-2, 18**
   other pronouns/substitute words
      both (Both are big.) **14**
      one – ones (the big one/ones) **14**
      the other – the others **14**

Relative clauses: see *adjective clauses*

Quantifiers
   both (both ears) **18**
   each **18**
   a few **3**
   any (any hair) **16**
   a lot of **14**
   lots of **14**
   no (no hair) **18**
   some **3**

Questions and Answers **A-3**

There is/ there are
   there is **3**
   there are **3**

Bibliography and Additional Resources
Simple classroom drawings

Garcia, Ramiro. *The Graphics Book.* Los Gatos: Sky Oaks Productions, 1990.

Shapiro, Norma, and Carol Genser. *Chalk Talks.* Berkeley: Command Performance Language Institute, 1994.

Silvers, Stephen M. Drawing out language: Using drawings to develop listening and speaking. *English Teaching Professional 114* (January) 2018.

Wright, Andrew. *1000 + Pictures for Teachers to Copy.* New York: Pearson ELT, 1994.

TPR

Asher, James J. *Learning Another Language through Actions.* 7th ed. Los Gatos: Sky Oaks Productions, 2009.

Cabello, Francisco. *Total Physical Response in the first Year.* Sky Oaks Productions, 1985.

Garcia, Ramiro. *Instructor's Notebook: How to Apply TPR for Best Results.* 4th ed. Los Gatos: Sky Oaks Productions, 1996.

Seely, Contee and Elizabeth Romijn. *TPR is More Than Commands at All Levels.* 2nd ed. Berkeley: Command Performance Language Institute, 2001.

Silvers, Stephen M. *Listen and Perform.* Los Gatos: Sky Oaks Productions, 1985 (2nd ed., 1994).

Silvers, Stephen M. *Complete English Grammar on CD: The Best Way to TPR any Grammatical Feature in English.* Los Gatos: Sky Oaks Productions, 2013.

Silvers, Stephen M. A practical guide to actions in the classroom. *MEXTESOL Journal 39* (2), 2015.

Acknowledgements

I would like to acknowledge and thank those who have provided technical support and/or encouragement.

Dr. James J. Asher, the originator of TPR, has had a significant influence on all of my professional projects. My debt to him is quite substantial.

Josh Nollette, Self-publishing Coordinator at the University Book Store Press, the University of Washington, patiently and expertly guided me through the publishing process.

Jennifer Oleinik., a professional editor/proofreader in Seattle, spent many hours revising the mechanics, style, and layout. Her help is immensely appreciated.

Grace Rajendran, a talented artist in Seattle, produced the cover.

The **FEDEX team** at the Lake City store provided exceptionally good service for the printing and binding of the many "working versions."

Stan Levinson, a long-time friend and former ESL/EFL teacher, gave advice on several aspects as the work was being developed.

My brother, **Jeff,** and my sister, **Maureen,** gave constant and much appreciated encouragement.

My children, **Paula, Sergio,** and **David,** my son-in-law, **Thomas,** and my daughters-in-law, **Angela** and **Mirella,** are an inspiration and gave much support and encouragement.

Finally, my greatest thanks and appreciation go to my wife, **Neusa Maria,** who sadly is not here to share with me the completion of this project.

About the author

Stephen Mark "Gil" Silvers has a master's degree in Spanish from the University of California (UCLA). He has nearly forty years of classroom experience, having begun his career as a U.S. Information Agency English Teaching Fellow at the Manaus Brazilian-American Cultural Institute (ICBEU) in 1972. There, in addition to teaching, he was responsible (along with two other teachers) for the teacher-training courses.

From 1974 until 2003 he was an instructor in the Federal University of Amazonas's Department of Foreign Languages and Literatures, where he taught all levels of English as well as American literature and the methodology course for future English teachers.

From 2003 until 2010, he taught English to engineers at CT-PIM, a science and technology center for the Manaus industrial pole. There, with help from the company's computer department, he created and developed *ESL Station*, a website for EFL/ESL learners.

He was a presenter at the Twelfth Annual TESOL Convention in Mexico City and made presentations at various BRAZ-TESOL conventions and ENPULI conferences (a Brazilian national conference of university-level English teachers).

He is the author of *Listen and Perform; The Command Book*; *Point and Touch; Listen and Act* (special editions for the Amazonas state public schools); and *Complete English Grammar on CD: the Best Way to TPR any Grammatical Feature in English*.

He is retired and lives in Seattle where he continues to work on and develop EFL/ESL teaching materials.

www.ingramcontent.com/pod-product-compliance
Lightning Source LLC
Chambersburg PA
CBHW072049290426
44110CB00014B/1613